God's Love Story:

The Story of God's Love
In the Messiah's Life, Death, and Resurrection
Book 10

By R. Lane Lender

STORIES OF LIFE PRODUCTIONS

God's Love Story: The Story of God's Love in the Messiah's Life, Death, and Resurrection, Book 10

Copyright © 2020 By Stories of Life Productions

ISBN: 978-1-970032-17-8 (Hard Cover)

ISBN: 978-1-970032-46-8 (eBook)

For more information about Stories of Life Productions and/or God's Love Story Visual Bible visit www.glsvb.org.

All rights reserved. No part of this publication may be reproduced, stored in a retrieval system, or transmitted in any form or by any means – electronic, mechanical, photocopy, recording, or any other – except for brief quotations in printed reviews, without the prior permission of Stories of Life Productions.

Published in the United States of America

Introduction

God's Love Story Children's Book Series is dedicated to my grandchildren. One of the greatest gifts a parent can pass off to their children is a passion to love Jesus more than anything else in this world. This passion is more caught than taught. Our children need to see our love for Jesus and they too will follow in our footsteps. My wife and I are truly blessed to not only have godly parents but to have two wonderful children, now in their mid twenties, who have learned to love Jesus from birth. As I write, my son is a prosecuting attorney in Texas and my daughter is married to a wonderful man, a dedicated Christ follower. They now have one child and their hope is many more. My daughter is also preparing to homeschool them all like she and her brother were. My desire is to provide a biblically-based tool for parents to use to cultivate in their children a love for Jesus in their most precious and formative years. I desire nothing more than to see my future grandchildren come to know Jesus and to develop into solid Kingdom contributing Christ followers. Thus, I submit this contribution. My prayer is that this book series develops in your children a love for the gospel and a passion for Jesus.

I also want to thank you for your purchase of this book and the other books in this series (See the back cover for more details). Your purchase goes directly to support Stories of Life Productions as we continue to produce, promote, and distribute God's Love Story Visual Bible (GLSVB). GLSVB is an oral story Bible created for the cell phone that has been translated into several languages of Unreached People Groups (UPGs). These UPGs live in places that are very difficult to access with the gospel. Because of your purchase, as well as gifts from generous donors, GLSVB is provided free to missionaries and believers around the world who are using this tool for evangelism and discipleship. GLSVB can be accessed at www.hikayaat.com. To find out more information, order books, or help us promote God's Love Story Children's Book series or GLSVB, visit www.glsvb.org. May God's Love Story Children's Books give you and your child a passion to serve Christ and His Kingdom's purpose!

Sincerely,
R. Lane Lender
Stories of Life Productions
contact@glsvb.org
www.hikayaat.com
www.glsvb.org

We read in the gospels how our Lord Jesus, began His ministry;
At 30 years old, He came to the prophet, John the Baptist, the greatest, you see;

Near the River Jordan, proclaiming repentance,
"Turn from sin and misery!;
God will forgive you if you are sincere,
Giving life and victory!";

There Jesus was Baptized, obedient to God,
An example for us to follow;
Down in the river, up out of the water,
Our new life in Christ to show;

From there Jesus went to the wilderness,
For 40 days fasting and praying;
There Satan tempted but Jesus rejected,
Quoting scripture, on God's word He was staying;

One day, Jesus read a prophecy from Isaiah,
In the scriptures, it was of Him;
"Today this scripture is fulfilled in your hearing,"
Many were angry and grim;

For 3 years, they travelled to preach to the lost,
Healing and raising the dead;
The blind given sight, the outcast new life,
For in Jesus their sins were shed;

Great crowds would follow wher'er they went,
To see what Jesus would do;
Not all were happy with what He was doing
They watched with a jealous hue;

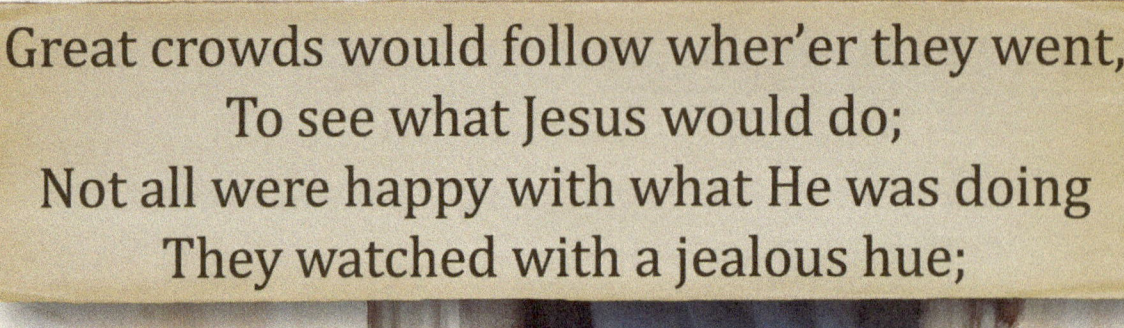

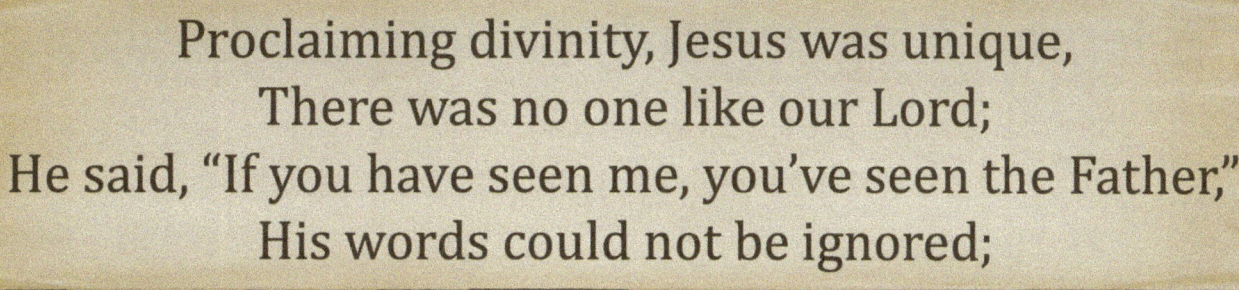

Proclaiming divinity, Jesus was unique,
There was no one like our Lord;
He said, "If you have seen me, you've seen the Father,"
His words could not be ignored;

Jesus did many miracles, no one could deny,
So powerful was He;
"Tabitha rise! Come back to life!"
Truly alive was she;

One day, Jesus and his disciples,
Were crossing the Lake Galilee;
A storm all the sudden came down upon them,
Jesus slept, the boat tossed by the sea;

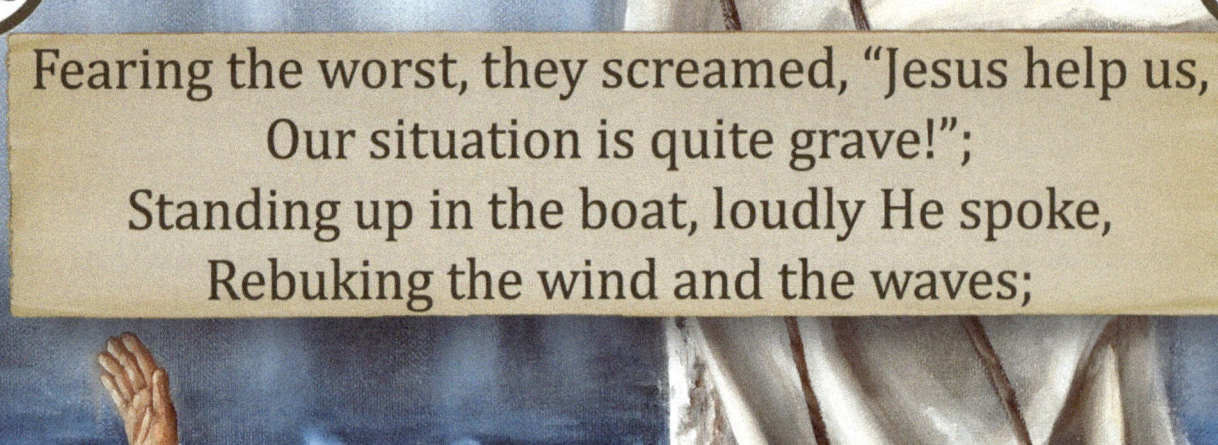

Fearing the worst, they screamed, "Jesus help us,
Our situation is quite grave!";
Standing up in the boat, loudly He spoke,
Rebuking the wind and the waves;

But Pilot balked at killing the Lord,
So he had Jesus beaten;
By our Lord's stripes we are healed,
Through Jesus, sin's power is broken;

The crowd won him over, taking Jesus away,
Pilate to them, relenting;
They led Jesus down the Via Dolorosa,
The way of suffering;

They hung Him to die, a horrible death,
Nails in His hands and feet;
Giving His all He said, "It is finished,"
The penalty of sin to defeat;

They lowered His body down to the ground,
With the Sabbath approaching fast;
A rich man named Joseph, prepared Jesus for burial,
With help from Nicodemus;

Laid in Joseph's tomb, hewn out of the rock,
With care they wrapped Him tight;
Before sundown, in a hurry they found,
Little time to do the job right;

After Sabbath's passing early Sunday morn',
The ladies went to the tomb;
To finish the job with spices in hand,
The tomb empty, they were gloom;

But Angels appeared saying, "Go tell the apostles,
That Jesus, He is alive!;
He has arisen, just as He said,"
So they ran with spirits revived;

They found the apostles with locked doors in fear,
Confusion and doubt still remained;
But the ladies insisted that He had arisen,
Investigating, their hearts still restrained;

Returning to the house for fear of the Jews,
They shut and locked all the doors;
Suddenly there, Jesus appeared,
What joy! They could not ignore;

For 40 days, Jesus appeared many times,
Reinforcing what they had learned;
Giving them the authority and the commission,
"Go make disciples of all the world";

Before He ascended into the heavens,
He told of the Spirit to come;
"Empowered by the Spirit, you'll be my witnesses,
To the ends of the earth" is the outcome;

Lightning Source UK Ltd.
Milton Keynes UK
UKHW050724190920
370074UK00004B/113

9 781970 032178